How to Boost Your Credit
100+ Points In 30 Days
WITHOUT
Credit Repair

FACT: Your payment history accounts for only 35% of your credit score. That leaves another 65% for you to optimize.

FACT: It's possible to have a credit score in the low 600's even if you paid every bill on time your entire life.

While most people obsess with removing late payments and collections to improve their credit scores, credit industry insiders secretly manipulate the other 4 credit factors to help their customers achieve huge credit score increases almost overnight.

Inside you will learn:

- ✓ Why the scores you buy online are worthless.
- ✓ How FICO scores are calculated.
- ✓ How to boost your score in 24 hours guaranteed!
- ✓ How to find credit cards with guaranteed approval.
- ✓ How to get an installment loan while still in bankruptcy.
- ✓ How to get collections deleted from your credit report.
- ✓ How to get lenders to remove a 30 day late.
- ✓ How to get credit card offers from the best lenders mailed to your home.
- ✓ When and how to open or close a credit card.
- ✓ A little known technique for paying off your credit card debt.
- ✓ And much much more!

Your 2 Free Gifts

As a thank you for buying this book, please enjoy these 2 free resources:

1) Free Audio Book Download
2) Free video case study of credit optimization performed on actual credit reports

Go to the link below to get instant access:

www.HowtoFixMyCredit.com/2freegifts

Brian Diez

CEO of Howtofixmycredit.com

Amazon Best Selling Author

Table of Content

Over the next 30 days you're going to learn strategies for boosting your credit score in record time.

We are going to focus on the little hinges, the smaller over looked details, that open big doors and create big change.

Day 1 - Get your credit scores.

Before you go signing up for just any old credit monitoring service, here's what you should know:

All credit scores are not the same.

Lenders currently use FICO05 scores.

But you, as a consumer, cannot purchase FICO05 scores.

In fact, the only way for you to see your FICO05 scores would be to apply for a home loan.

It's a little known fact that each monitoring service like TransUnion, FreeCreditReport.com, etc., sells their own scores.

They're made to look just like FICO scores, but they're not FICO.

Take a look for yourself:

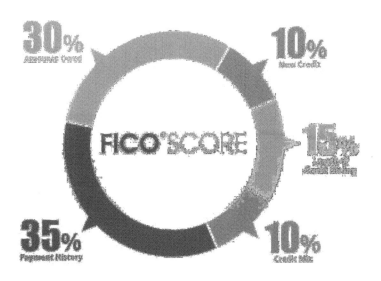

FICO uses a score range of 350-850.

All of the other scores use a similar range.

Why do they do this? To deceive you and take your money, of course.

They could've used any score range they wanted.

1-10, A-F, 100-500... but they purposely replicated a similar range so you wouldn't be able to tell the difference between their worthless scores and FICO.

So, if their scores are worthless and all the data is the same on each site, that tells us that you should not spend more for credit monitoring from a big brand name like TransUnion or Experian.

You should invest as little as possible, which is why I recommend using www.identityiqreport.com

You get all 3 bureau reports, plus worthless scores for just $1 for 7 days, then $19.99 a month.

You'll need to keep your account open throughout this process.

Day 2 - Take A Snap Shot

Today we're going to take a snap shot of your current credit file.

You'll want it organized so you can see the areas that need improvement.

Don't skip this step. It's crucial for your success.

This will help not only give you direction, but will also motivate you to stick to your plan.

Use Google spreadsheets or Excel and make 5 columns.

Label each column Lender, Limit, Balance, Utilization, Date Opened, and whether its opened or closed.

Underneath you'll list your revolving accounts. These include credit cards, retail cards, charge cards, and secured cards.

For example:

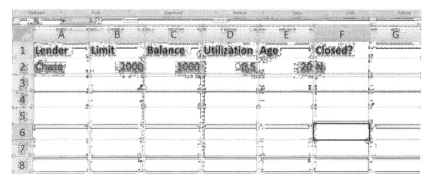

On a second sheet you'll repeat the process for your installment accounts.

Installment accounts include loans, auto, and home financing.

Be sure to list all your accounts, even the closed ones.

You'll use this as a reference for future lessons.

Day 3 - How FICO Scores Are Calculated

For some this may be basic information, but it needs to be addressed to ensure we're all on the same page.

Let's take at FICO scores and how they're calculated.

Your FICO score is a numerical representation of the odds that a consumer will default 90 days or more on a credit card or loan.

That's really all it is.

The lender wants to know what the odds are that you'll stop paying for 3 months or more.

Here is the breakdown:

800+	1485 to 1
720-799	659 to 1
680-719	112 to 1
620-679	47 to 1
Below 620	15 to 1

That means for every 47 consumers with 625 scores they lend money to, on average 1 will default by 90 days.

That means for the lender to make money, they have to charge more interest to those with lower scores to offset the losses of the 1 who defaulted.

How your scores are calculated are based on 5 criteria:

1) Payment history (35%) - do you pay your accounts on time
2) Amounts owed (30%) - how much of your credit are you using out of your available credit
3) Length of credit history (15%) - how old are your accounts? Generally, older is better

4) Credit mix in use (10%) - what's your ratio of credit cards, retail accounts, installment loans, finance company accounts and mortgage loans
5) New credit (10%) - Opening several credit accounts in a short period of time represents a greater risk - especially for people who don't have a long credit history.

This information, when combined with your spreadsheet from yesterday, will help you start to see the areas of your credit that are the easiest to improve.

Before we get into that, we have one more thing to discuss... FICO score cards.

Day 4 - FICO Score Cards

In the FICO scoring formula, not all credit reports are scored equally.

Credit scores are Weighted based on the particular "score card" that a person falls under.

For example, if the person has filed for bankruptcy, they may be scored using a special "bankruptcy" scorecard.

The credit score for a person under one scorecard may be affected differently by s negative event, like a late payment, then of someone with the same event on a different scorecard.

The score card you're on is determined by the most recent significant event in your credit history.

The first 10 scorecards go something like this...

Scorecards 1-5:

1. Those with public records, including judgements and bankruptcy, on their credit report
2. For those with serious delinquencies other than bankruptcies (60, 90, 120 lates, collections, judgments, charge-offs repossessions, etc.).
3. Those with only 1 credit account (very thin files)
4. Those with only 2 credit accounts (thin files)
5. Those with only 3 credit accounts.

Scorecards 6-10 must NOT have ANY serious delinquencies (the definition of "serious" is unknown)

6. 0-2 years oldest account

7. 2-5 years oldest account

8. 5-12 years oldest account

9. 12-19 years oldest account

10. 19+ years oldest account

There are a total of 12 score cards, and they are subject to change as FICO (formerly Fair Isaac Corp) updates their scoring formula.

Day 5 - How Score Cards Effect Your Scores

Just a quick recap...

1. You got a recent credit report and got smart about not overpaying for credit scores.
2. You put all your tradelines on a spreadsheet and got yourself organized.
3. You learned why banks use FICO scores and how they're calculated.
4. And you learned about FICO score cards and how they affect your scores.

How you score is based on how you compare to 1.5 million other people on your same score card as they're tracked over a period of 2 years.

For example, let's say you're on a bankruptcy score card.

If FICO tracks 1.5M people who were recently discharged from bankruptcy, and of those people 75% of those that had a 30 day late in the first 6 months ended up defaulting 90 days or more, then it's safe to say that a 30 day late will crush your score if it happens in the first 6 months.

If the average person who is discharged from bankruptcy has no open credit cards, and you have 3 with great history and high limits, then your score will be better than average.

Using the score cards and spreadsheet from you last lessons, try to figure out which card you're on.

Next you'll need to use some common sense to figure out what it would take to better than average on your score card OR what it would take to get a different score card.

For example, if you're on a thin credit score card you probably only have 1 or 2 credit cards and the age of your credit report is very new.

If you added an older account, that would age your credit file and boost your score.

If you added an installment loan, that would improve your credit mix.

Get the idea?

Make a quick list and over the next several lessons I'll teach you Yoda-like techniques for manipulating the FICO formula.

Day 6 - How Many Credit Cards Should You Have?

Not all credit is the same.

Credit cards, for example, carry more weight than installment loans.

The right credit card can improve your credit almost overnight.

While you do need to mix up your credit, credit cards show lenders how responsible you are on a monthly basis.

VISA and MasterCard are the 2 big players in this area.

Believe it or not, people who don't have a major credit card are considered a bigger credit risk than people with 14 credit cards.

Without a bank credit card, your credit score will never be as high as it could be.

In fact, to truly optimize your credit scores you should have between 2-4 bank credit cards.

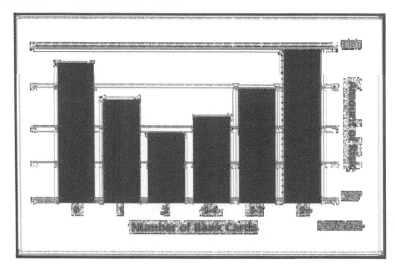

If FICO is saying that 2-4 is optimal, then it's your job to make it so.

In order to fully realize the benefits of your 2 credit cards you also need age and a high limit.

Age will come in time., but you can speed the limit building side of the equation.

If your score is over 700, then you should call and request a credit limit increase at least once every 6-9 months.

If your score is under 700, then you might want to start with a secure credit card.

Start out with a $500 limit and work to building that limit to $5,000.

Once you hit $5,000, then open a second secure card and do it again.

Day 7 - Add Or Close Your Retail Cards

Retail cards are those provided by the stores where you shop.

Target, The Home Depot, and Kohls are 3 very popular ones.

You want 1 or 2 retail cards on your credit for the sake of your credit mix.

Close accounts if you have more than 2.

Before you close an account, just be sure it's not your oldest tradeline and that the balance is zero.

Another thing to consider is that retail cards won't help you if you never use them.

A lender suddenly closing your account due to inactivity can drop your score.

Just make sure to keep your balances under 10% and never keep balances on all your cards at the same time.

Day 8 - What You Need to Know About Public Records

Your credit report has 4 sections.

1. Personal data
2. Credit history
3. Inquiries
4. Public records

There is no positive listing that can appear in your public records section.

In fact, any listing that appears here might as well be a bankruptcy.

You have to watch this area of your credit report closely.

In many cases, creditors and collection agents are able to obtain a judgement against you without your knowledge.

One day, you just find a lien on your credit report.

Of course, this isn't legal, but most people don't know that.

You would need to find an attorney and get the judgement vacated on the grounds that you were never served.

Everyone has the right to defend themselves in court.

If you were served, then it may still be possible to remove the record, but that would require disputing.

Just know that it's all but impossible to score in the 800's with a public record on your credit report.

Day 9 - Pay Down Your Debt

It's no secret that having less debt is better for your credit scores.

But there's a right and wrong way to pay down your debt.

Some financial experts will tell you to pay off your mortgage and car first.

While this may be a good strategy when it comes to planning for your future, it isn't ideal for your credit scores.

Bottom line, there is debt you want to pay down and there is debt you want to keep open.

There are two main types of credit accounts: Revolving Credit and Installment Loans

Installment loans basically mean you are paying a fixed amount over a predetermined period of time.

Auto loans, mortgages, and personal loans fall into this category.

With installment loans you want to make consistent payments for the full course of the loan.

Paying an installment account off faster will not improve your credit much, if at all.

Revolving credit is a different animal entirely.

Any debt where your balances can fluctuate up or down from month to month are considered revolving.

This includes credit cards like Visa, MasterCard, American Express and Discover.

You want to pay down your debt quickly to optimize your credit scores.

The reason is simple; with revolving debt the risk is greater to the lender because you generally don't have an underlying asset as collateral.

Go back to your spreadsheet and ensure you have all your accounts in their proper columns.

Focus your attention on paying down your revolving credit. Leave the installment accounts alone.

Day 10 - How to Pay Down Debt

Knowing which revolving debts to pay off first matters.

I'm going to cover 2 different approaches.

Which you choose will depend on your need and how well you know yourself.

The first approach I call the Snow Ball method.

This is the approach I use personally because I know I need to see results quickly or I will lose interest.

Here's how it works...

List your revolving debt in order of lowest balance to highest balance.

Make the minimum payment on all your credit cards except the one with the lowest balance.

Any extra income you have is used to pay down this balance first.

Once the card is paid off, then take that same money you were using to pay the first card off and use it to pay down the second card.

This works because you have larger and larger sums of money to knock your debt down.

From a psychological point of view, it's very rewarding to see cards with zero balances accumulating as well as having larger and larger sums of money to drive your next balance down.

While extremely effective, the Snow Ball method is not the best method for improving your FICO scores.

Most people assume that paying down the card with the highest interest rate would be the next logical step, but that's incorrect.

You need to think like FICO and understand what FICO considers important.

When calculating your credit scores, FICO takes four criteria into consideration:

1. Overall combined utilization
2. Line item utilization
3. Number of accounts with a balance
4. Number of highly utilized credit cards

Utilization just means how much of your credit you're using.

For example, if your credit card balance is $500 and your limit is $1000, then your utilization is 50%.

Utilization is the most heavily weighted factor when it comes to your revolving debt.

Your overall combined utilization is the total of all of your revolving accounts' credit limits, compared to the balance you owe on those same accounts.

So, let's say you have 10 credit cards, each with a $1,000 limit. Your total revolving credit limit is $10,000. Now let's say 6 of those cards are maxed out. This leaves you with $4,000 of available credit (meaning that you are 60% utilized).

Your line item utilization is for each individual credit account.

So if you have a Chase credit card with a $1500 limit and you have a $1500 balance, then you are 100% utilized on this account.

The number of your credit card accounts with a balance is just like it sounds.

It's good to have credit cards, but it's even better to have credit cards with a zero balance.

If you are close to maxing them out, FICO will adjust your credit score accordingly.

Once you know what FICO deems as important, it becomes easier for you to create a strategy to properly pay off revolving debt.

Take out your spreadsheet again.

First you'll want to pay off any cards that have low balances on them. Remember that using too many cards is not a good thing, so always keep at least one card at zero.

Next you'll list your lenders in order of highest utilization to lowest.

For example:

Your Pay-off Priority List should look like this:

1. Citibank
2. US Bank
3. Macy's
4. Shell
5. Sears

Citibank is first because the amount owed is small... and having a credit card account with a zero balance will increase your score.

The other revolving credit cards' order was based on the utilization percentage of each card.

This is how you hack FICO's scoring formula to optimize your credit scores.

You will start to see a credit score increase in about 30-40 days.

Lenders only update their records with the credit bureaus once a month.

The date they update is normally about 10 days after your due date.

It's important to note that using your credit cards while you're paying them down is counter-productive.

Day 11 - Zero Balance Letter

Here's a slick trick for realizing a faster credit score increase after you pay off each credit card.

It's called a Zero Balance letter.

1. Confirm your last payment cleared with your bank.
2. Contact the customer service department of the credit card company and tell them you are applying for a home loan and need a "Zero Balance" letter.

They may insist on mailing it, but try to get them to fax it to you instead. There are dozens of websites that will give you a free fax number and up to 10 free faxes a month. eFax.com for example.

Once you have your letter in hand, simply mail it to each of the 3 bureaus. Your records will be updated in about 2 weeks.

Want to speed up the process even more? Here's what you need to do:

Apply for a home loan.

If you don't have a trusted mortgage consultant, then email me at brian@howtofixmycredit.com and I'll set you up with mine.

Now you have 2 options.

Option 1: Your mortgage lender can perform a rapid rescore. They will provide the third party credit service they used to pull your credit with your Zero Balance letter.

The third party will instantly update their records and notify the credit bureaus of the change.

The credit bureaus will reflect the change in about 24 hours.

Your mortgage consultant may charge you for a rapid rescore.

Option 2: Contact the credit bureaus directly. Tell them you're applying for a home loan and need to fax a zero balance letter.

They will give you an unpublished number after they verify the mortgage inquiry on your credit report.

Check your score in about 48 hours and you will see the change.

Note: Yes, a mortgage inquiry will hurt your score, but the zero balance letter will more than offset the inquiry.

Besides, you're only doing a pre-qualification. You won't actually be submitting your application to lenders who would each need to pull a copy of your credit during underwriting.

Using this process, you may realize a huge credit score increase in 24-48 hours from start to finish.

Day 12 - Reviving Old Accounts

Another often overlooked strategy for improving your credit scores is to reactivate old accounts that were in good standing when they closed.

I see it all the time.

Someone closed an old account because they weren't using it and their scores dropped.

Other times a creditor closes an account due to inactivity.

In either case, it's sometimes possible to reopen the account and recapture the benefit of the older tradeline.

Often these accounts can be reactivated, even if they've been closed for several years, with just a phone call.

This can be a good, low-key and cheap way for you to a) add to your "high credit limit", b) improve your debt-to-credit ratio, c) increase the average age of your revolving accounts, d) all while getting another "good" account added to your credit report.

Day 13 - Increase Your Credit Limits

One of the least utilized strategies for lowering your debt utilization is a credit limit increase.

All you need to do is call your lender and ask if a credit limit increase is available for your account.

In fact, I just called Capital One this morning to inquire about changing my account from cash rebate to an account that earns miles.

They told me both my accounts qualified for upgrades. They dropped my interest rate, increased my rebate on one card, and changed the second to one that earns me miles.

Most people don't know that a customer service rep will pull up your entire account before they even answer the phone.

They use caller ID to identify you, then have you prove your identity.

Once proven, they have all your past conversations, your limits, balances, and possible upgrades available.

They just won't tell you unless you ask.

By requesting a credit limit increase you're effectively increasing your available credit without increasing your balance.

For example, if you have one card with a $500 limit and $250 balance, then you're at 50% utilization.

If you get a $500 limit increase, then you have $1000 limit with a $250 balance. That brings your utilization down to only 25% instantly!

The lower your utilization, the higher your scores.

With a secured card you simply increase your deposit.

For a regular credit card, make sure you make timely payments for at least 6 months, though 9 months is better.

Make sure you keep your card under 50% utilization on all your cards.

They won't approve you if you're maxed out or have missed payments within the past year.

If they ask you what you're going to use the money for, don't say gambling, or anything irresponsible.

Say you're trying to improve your FICO scores or that you just got a raise and wanted to buy some new furniture.

If they ask how large an increase you would like, ask them how much you qualify for.

They can tell you after a minute or so.

If you're approved, then you just raised your credit scores with a phone call.

Day 14 - Become an Authorized User

A very simple yet effective technique for boosting your credit scores it to "piggyback" on someone else's credit history and become an Authorized User (AU) on their account.

An AU account is not like a Joint Account.

With a Joint Account both you and the primary holder can add to the credit balance, but you're also both liable for the debts.

If, for example, the primary files for bankruptcy protection, then you will be on the hook for the full balance.

You should avoid Joint accounts at all costs.

With an Authorized User account, only the primary card holder is liable for the debt.

However, the tradeline appears on BOTH credit reports.

This is a great way to start your children's credit education, too.

The overnight addition to a credit's age, limit, and payment history can boost a score hundreds of points.

AU accounts are so effective for boosting credit scores that many unscrupulous credit services actually sell them as "Seasoned Tradelines".

First of all, buying a tradeline for the purpose of qualifying for financing, like a home mortgage, is fraud. You could go to jail or receive a hefty fine.

Second, FICO knows about Seasoned Tradelines and has made adjustments. When those adjustments hit the scoring model lenders use, then those tradelines will become worthless.

Third, you don't need to buy tradelines anyway. Simply ask a family member, or someone you've shared an address with, to add you as an AU.

Tell them you don't need or want a card, but you want your credit score to benefit from their good credit history.

Look for a card from a major lender with a high limit, low balance, and perfect payment history. The older the card the better.

Day 15 - Refinance Revolving Debt

Anytime you pay off your credit cards your score is going to go up.

Refinancing your revolving debt with an installment loan is a way to game the system into thinking you have less debt.

FICO doesn't give as much weight to installment loans, so adding the equivalent installment debt while paying off revolving debt will have an overall positive effect on your score.

Where do you go for installment loans when you have damaged credit?

I use 2 sites:

Avant.com (http://bit.ly/poor-credit-personal-loans)

Lendingclub.com

They specialize in exactly these types of loans.

Just don't go running up your cards while you're paying off your installment loan, or you'll end up with twice the debt.

That's a recipe for disaster.

Day 16 - Refinance Revolving Debt With a Home Equity Loan

Using a Home Equity Loan (HEL) to pay off your revolving debts will improve your credit scores for the same reason using any other installment loan to pay off your revolving debt would work.

FICO gives less weight to installment loan debt.

You just need to make sure you use a Home Equity LOAN and not a Home Equity Line of Credit (HELOC).

A HELOC is scored just like a credit card by FICO, so using it wouldn't improve your scores.

So if you have a HEL, or qualify for one, then this is a viable strategy for you.

Just be sure to use it to pay down your debt and not as a way to get yourself into more debt.

If you're not disciplined enough to not run up your balances again, then this would not be a smart move for you.

I include it because it works, but you have to pick and choose what works for YOU.

Day 17 - Credit Builder Loans

Some lenders offer a secured loan program designed to help you rebuild your credit.

They're called Credit Builder Loans.

This is a very effective, all be it slow, method for boosting your scores.

It's slower because it's an installment loan. Installment loans have less of an impact on your credit score.

Be that as it may, over 6-12 months you will see a credit score increase.

That's because you need a few installment loans to improve the "Credit Mix" which is responsible for 10% of your credit score.

Here's how your scores are determined:

FICO SCORES IMAGE

My ideal ratio is:

2-4 credit cards

A car loan, home loan, and personal loan

1-2 retail cards

The credit builder loan completes the personal loan portion of the equation.

Here's how it works...

The amount you borrow is deposited into an escrow account.

You can't touch it until the loan is paid.

You make your regular payments each month, building your credit score as you go.

When you're done paying, you get the full balance plus interest, to do with as you please.

Traditional features include:

Loan amounts from $500-$3000

12-24 month terms

Loan funds earn dividends

Loan interest rate is fixed at 5%

So, for example, a $1000 loan at 5% over 18 months would equal payments of $57.79.

The terms may change from bank to bank, so you need to shop around.

Here's one you can use for comparison: https://www.dcu.org/loans/credit-builder.html

Day 18 - Goodwill Letter

The goal of 100 Points in 30 Days is to find the small changes that have a big effect on your score without disputing with the credit bureaus.

In the next few lessons we'll look at some passive strategies for improving your payment history.

A Goodwill letter is a request you make to a creditor based on your past and future relationship.

I would only recommend using a Goodwill letter for a 1x30 day late in which the creditor may believe there was a billing or processing error.

Here's a sample letter:

Dear Creditor,

I recently reviewed my credit report and noticed a 30 day late reported back in 2010.

I have always paid my bills on time and do not recall any instance where it may have been late.

If you review my account history, you will see that this is the only lateness reported and I believe that this must be an error of some kind.

I value my credit score as much as my relationship with your company. I've been a happy customer for many years and would like to remain one.

Based on our relationship I ask that you remove this error as a matter of "good faith" based on the likelihood that it is probably an error of some kind.

Thanks in advance for your help.

Sincerely,

Customer

If you do decide to send a letter like this one, do not dispute the error with the bureaus first. You might inadvertently make them "dig in" to defend their remarks.

If the good will letter fails, then you can try disputing.

Day 19 - Hardship Letter

Think of a hardship letter as an extreme goodwill letter. This letter is used when you have several late payments, or are behind on payments, and can bring the account current.

In essence, you're asking for a little compassion. Terrible things happen all the time. We all need a break now and again.

Here is a sample letter:

Dear [creditor],

I have recently suffered a serious financial hardship when {spouse died, medical emergency, job loss, business failure, natural disaster... describe the hardship here in moderate detail.}

As a result of this hardship, I have fallen behind on my account with you and would like to do what I can to remedy the situation.

I have {x} late payments on my credit report as a result of this. I am writing to ask, as a matter of good faith, if you would remove the late payments on this account if I can bring the account current and pay all associated late fees.

I would like to salvage my credit and my relationship with you as a creditor as I've been a loyal customer for {x} years!

Any help you can provide, or any other options you may have, are very much appreciated.

Sincerely,

Customer

While we tend to think of lenders as big unfeeling machines we need to remember that there are caring and feeling people running those machines.

People can be reasoned with provided you have a real hardship.

Besides, lenders don't make money by sending your account to collections. Give them a reason to work with you and you might be surprised by the results.

Day 20 - Prove It

Obvious as it may seem, it still needs to be said. One of the most effective ways to boost your credit scores is to prove the credit bureaus made a mistake.

This is very different than disputing.

When you dispute, you are asking the credit bureaus and your creditors to prove they are correct. It's a long and tedious process, but effective nonetheless.

But there are times when you catch an error you can prove.

For example:

In this video I show you how I removed a mortgage late for a client who had actually paid on time. He had paid the principal, but not the interest. Since they accepted the payment, it couldn't be late.

http://www.howtofixmycredit.com/how-to-delete-a-30-day-late/

Other similar occurrences I come across often include:

A utility bill sent to collection that was paid in full and you can provide the canceled check.

Someone else's name or address appearing on your credit.

The same account appearing multiple times on your credit report with the same bureau.

A credit card reporting as closed by grantor when it was closed by the customer.

A student loan reported late when it was in deferment.

A car that was repossessed and sold at auction still reporting the full balance owed.

These are just a few examples that I see happen again and again.

When you find a legitimate error you have to:

Locate the proof to validate your case

Get the company to do the leg work and find their own error

A canceled check to prove the payment was made as well as the date it was processed is always a great form of proof.

With the mortgage payment above I had to call and get them to look into their own records to find the proof themselves.

When you get them to accept they were wrong, make sure you get a letter admitting the mistake.

Send the letter to the credit bureaus so they can update your file.

Always keep a copy of your proof and all your correspondence with your creditors.

Personally, I scan or fax documents to myself and keep a file in my Gmail account for each lender.

Evernote is also great for this, too.

And if the credit bureaus don't cooperate, then you always have howtofixmycredit.com to help you out.

After all, if it were easy, then I'd be in a different business.

Day 21 - Pay For Deletion

Once your lender writes off your debt, it is usually sold to a collection agency.

If they can't collect on the debt, then they'll sell it to yet another collection agency.

Whatever they collect over and above what they paid for the debt is their profit.

And debt can sell for mere pennies on the dollar.

As your debt gets bought and sold, the only record of your account is what's on their spreadsheet.

A collection agency doesn't get $10M worth of paperwork when they buy $10M worth of debt.

Unfortunately, collections can destroy your credit score.

And paying them off won't do you much good either.

According to FICO the only things that matter when it comes to a collection is:

Is there a collection?

When was it reported

Paying it off does nothing to help your score.

Once it's on there, it'll stay on there for 7 years.

The good news is the impact to your score diminishes over time.

But still, who wants to wait 7 years?

An alternative to waiting is to offer payment in exchange for deletion.

If it's deleted, then it is worth paying, because it no longer hurts your score.

There are many scenarios where this might apply, but I can't go through them all here. Let's just use the most common scenario.

Here's how it works...

Section 809(a) of the Fair Debt Collection Practices Act says certain disclosures are required "within five days after the initial communication with a consumer in connection with the collection of any debt."

Section 803(2) says that If the debt collector reports the collection account without first communicating with the consumer directly, then the consumer could reasonably consider the credit reporting itself to be an INDIRECT COMMUNICATION with the consumer THROUGH THE CREDIT BUREAU.

So if the first time you learned about a collection was seeing it on your credit report, then the credit bureau was the communication medium used by the collector for the initial communication.

If that's the case, then you have not received the proper disclosures as provided by Sec 809.

Did I lose you? Don't worry. Just send this letter:

"Dear [collector],

I was reviewing my credit report and was shocked to find a collection in the amount of $xx being reported by your company.

I have no idea what this collection is about.

Furthermore, it appears you have violated the law which states that you are supposed to notify me of a few things within 5 days of your initial communication.

I did not get that notification from you, so it is my understanding you are in violation of the Fair Debt Collection Practices Act.

While I do not believe this debt is mine, it is such a small amount that I am willing to PAY it in exchange for the REMOVAL of this entry from my credit report.

It is my opinion that this should never have been reported, and I think we can both agree that it will be easier for all of us if I can simply pay the amount due in exchange for the prompt removal of this item from my credit report.

Please respond in writing and let me know if you will accept my offer.

Sincerely,

Consumer

Note that you're not actually accusing anyone. You are only suggesting that they may be in violation.

No legal action is threatened.

I would only use this with new collections that you can pay in full.

Day 22 - Get Approved For New Credit

Another strategy for boosting your score by lowering your debt ratio and improving your credit mix is to add a new credit card.

I was working with a client not so long ago.

He was self-employed and trying to buy a house.

Actually, he was building a $1.5M home in Colorado.

The lender said he needed a 720 FICO to qualify for that type of construction loan.

Although he had never missed a payment, his scores were only around 680.

When I looked at his credit I realized the problem.

He had no credit cards.

He told me he only used an AMEX black card.

That's a charge card where you have to pay the balance in full each month.

And it doesn't show on your credit report unless you're late.

I had him add 2 new credit cards. He got both with $5,000 limits through Chase.

Within the next 45 days his scores all jumped to over 800.

When you're building credit, it's wise to focus on just 2 revolving accounts.

Work to building your credit limits up to at least $5,000 each.

You may have to start with a card that charges an annual fee.

That's OK as long as it's with a major lender.

Over time, they'll drop the fees and upgrade your account.

Just follow the strategies I taught you in the lesson about increasing your credit limits.

2 revolving bank cards and 1-2 retail cards.

Just make sure you don't shop around or the inquiries will drag your score down.

A good site for finding out where to apply is this one:

https://creditboards.com/forums/index.php?app=creditpulls

Also, you can opt-in to start receiving credit offers here:

https://www.optoutprescreen.com/opt_form.cgi

Day 23 - Removing Inquiries

Inquiries are a record of requests to see your credit report.

There are 2 types; hard and soft.

A hard inquiry occurs when your credit is pulled in connection with a firm credit offer. So if you apply for a mortgage or credit card, that's a hard inquiry.

Hard inquiries make up 10% of your credit score. They will remain on your credit for 2 years, but really only effect your score the first year.

In order to obtain a credit report on a person, the person or company pulling your credit must have "permissible purpose".

Your written authorization is the most common permissible purpose.

Some others include employment, underwriting insurance, or a court order.

Removing hard inquiries is usually a matter of requesting the permissible purpose or claiming they had none and demanding an explanation.

Generally, you contact the creditor or collection agency directly. The credit bureaus will tell you to go direct, as well.

Here is a sample letter:

Re: Unauthorized Credit Inquiry

Dear [Creditor],

While reviewing a recent copy of my [Experian, TransUnion or Equifax] credit report I noticed a credit inquiry by your company that I do not recall authorizing.

Please have this inquiry removed from my credit file as soon as possible, since I have no recollection of authorizing your inquiry. I have sent this letter certified mail because I need your prompt response to this issue.

I would greatly appreciate receiving a written response that you have had the unauthorized inquiry removed.

If you find that I am mistaken, and can provide written authorization and permissible purpose, then please send me proof of both.

Thanks in advance,

[Your Name]

[SSN]

Day 24 - Correcting Merged Data

A client of mine was a bail bondsman.

While I was assisting him with his initial credit audit, he asked me what my cell phone number was.

I gave it to him.

His next question was, "how long have you had this number?"

I told him, "About 15 years."

He explained that criminals use pre-pay track phones and always have a new number.

Apparently, my having the same phone for 15 years was very reassuring that I wouldn't steal his money and disappear.

This also applies to your credit report.

Look at the number of "aliases", prior addresses, and employers on your credit report.

Do you look like a solid credit risk, or do you look like someone who lies about their name, moves around a lot, and can't hold a job?

What's worse is this data might result in the merge of data from another credit file.

The bureaus refer to aliases, addresses, SSN variations, etc., as "additional sources of information".

There are several reasons they occur...

Typos

Someone with a similar name's info was merged to yours

spouse's info being mixed with yours

People with common names living at the same residence

Removing that additional data is usually easy.

Just send this letter:

> Dear [credit Bureaus]
>
> An additional source of information is being reported to my credit report.
>
> I request this source be removed.
>
> Specifically, anything tied to the "alias" x, previous address x, SSN x...
>
> These are not mine.
>
> Thank you.
>
> Sincerely,
>
> Consumer

Any data that was merged as a result of the "additional sources of data" should drop off as well.

Day 25 - Subprime Financing

Yet another strategy for instantly establishing revolving credit, lowering your debt utilization, and improving your credit mix is through the use of subprime credit.

Subprime is a double edged sword.

The pros:

You can get credit lines instantly of up to $5000

No credit check

99.9% approval rate

Usually results in a large credit score improvement

The cons:

A subprime financing company appears on your credit.

In many cases, they only report to 2 out of 3 bureaus.

They tend to carry hefty application and processing fees

You can only use them for the specific store associated with the account

Many mortgage lenders will require a minimum of 3 active tradelines with a $1500 limit to qualify for home financing.

For some that can be difficult.

It's in these situations that I most often rely on subprime accounts.

My favorite is:

http://bit.ly/myjewelersclub

* $5,000 Unsecured Revolving Line of Credit

* Reports to all 3 Bureaus

* Fully Refundable Processing fee if not approved.

MyJewelersClub.com does a good job of staying compliant with credit guidelines

and that keeps them from getting booted from being able to report.

Day 26 - Opt-in/Opt-out to Credit Marketing

The credit bureaus regularly rent information to lenders for marketing purposes.

You can capitalize on this opportunity and get pre-screened offers mailed to you.

Here's how it works...

Let's say, Chase, wants to sell more prime credit card accounts to balance out their portfolio.

They may reach out to Experian to rent a list of home owners, age 34-54, with 3 or more credit cards, living in California, that have 700-740 scores.

Experian then rents them that list of names, addresses, phone numbers, etc.

Chase can now mail "pre-qualified" or "pre-approved" offers to that list based on the information they've rented.

Remember, you want 2 revolving credit cards and no more.

People who have too many credit cards can opt-out of such offers to reduce their temptation of opening more accounts.

People looking to build credit can opt-in, since they're more likely to get approved.

Whether you're opting in or out, the website is the same:

https://www.optoutprescreen.com

Opting out lasts for 5 years, unless you physically opt back in.

Day 27 - Use Your Debit Card

Over the next few lessons we're going to discuss various strategies for reducing your debt utilization while trying to build your scores.

The first is to use your debit card.

As you have learned by now, the higher your revolving balance, the lower your scores.

While you may be trying some of the strategies in this course to lower your debt utilization, all your hard work is meaningless if you run up your balances again.

One way to keep your balances down is to start using your debit card instead of your credit card for daily transactions.

While your debit card doesn't offer you the same protection or rewards, it is a temporary solution that will help you maintain a low balance just until you reach your credit goals.

Day 28 - Use a Charge Card

A charge card is very different from a credit card.

With a charge card you must pay your entire balance in full at the end of each month.

That also means you don't pay interest either.

There are many benefits to using a charge card.

First, historically speaking, charge cards don't show on your personal credit report.

No balance to report means it won't hurt your debt utilization.

Another benefit to using a charge card is protection for your purchases.

If you place an order with your charge card and it arrives damaged, or significantly different than advertised, just call your lender and have the charges reversed.

Besides protecting your purchases, you are also personally protected.

I once purchased some software by phone.

A week later I got a call from AMEX asking me if I had purchased a Range Rover and a BMW in Maryland.

I hadn't.

Apparently, the cleaning lady had helped herself to my credit card information.

She and her friends thought they'd go on a shopping spree.

I had an AMEX black card at the time and placed everything from my mortgage payments to my phone bill on that card.

AMEX jumped on the situation, reversed the charges, and sent me a new card.

It was painless.

AMEX is my favorite charge card because it comes with lots of great features.

For example, your AMEX gets you access to the Captain's Room, which is great if you have a layover at an airport.

Some of their cards come with a concierge service.

Just tell your concierge what you need and they'll find it for you at no additional cost to you.

Some cards offer travel miles, rebates, or a points program where you can claim free gifts.

There's nothing better than planning a trip and finding out the airfare is free.

My point is a charge card is far better than paying with your debit card.

Get one as soon as you can qualify.

Day 29 - Use a Business Credit Card

Another way to prevent your FICO scores from taking a nose dive is to use a business credit card instead of your personal credit cards.

Business credit card balances don't show on your personal credit unless you 1) personally guarantee them and 2) miss payments.

Therefore, any purchases made with a business credit card will not adversely affect your scores.

Even if you max out your business credit card month after month, it will not hurt your personal credit score.

Unfortunately, the balances you carry with your PERSONAL credit cards effects your scores more than almost anything else.

[Read that last sentence again.]

While you still should carry at least 2 personal credit cards, for credit building purposes, they don't necessarily need to be your primary cards.

Not sure how to go about getting approved for business credit cards?

Check out my Business Credit Blueprint program:

http://loans4success.com

You'll learn everything from how and why to establish a corporation to where to get approved for business credit cards without a personal guarantee.

Day 30 - What to do if your scores go down.

Your credit score is nothing more than a statistical representation of your credit report.

And your credit report is a snapshot of your credit history at this moment in time.

If your score drops, then it's because something has changed on your credit report.

It's a dynamic process that happens instantaneously.

One of the most frustrating things about understanding your credit score is trying to figure out what happened when something good happened on your credit report, like a negative deleted or you added a new account, but your score dropped.

When this happens, the answer is likely that you changed score cards.

If you really want to find out what happened, then here's what you need to do:

1) Print out your current credit report
2) Compare it to a previous credit report
3) Highlight any changes made on the new report, line by line, bureau by bureau

Go back and review the highlighted areas and try to figure out how each change may have effected your score.

Once you have some educated guesses, the solution will present itself.

Here are 9 of the most common changes that could cause your score to drop:

Late payment

Collection

Increased balance on revolving debt

New credit inquiries

A new account

A credit limit was lowered

A credit limit is not reporting

An account was closed

Something previously "in-dispute" is no longer in-dispute status

My best advice would be to sign up with www.identityiqreport.com so you get emailed notifications of any negative changes to your credit report.

You will also see the effect of those changes, so you can begin to understand which events have the biggest impact.

It's a challenge that never gets old... and I've been doing it since 2006.

Made in the USA
Middletown, DE
19 July 2019